the lonely hearts club

Julie + Stella ♡

THANK YOU _SO_ MUCH
FOR SUPPORTING ME.
I HOPE THESE WORDS HELP
YOU AS MUCH AS THEY'VE
HELPED ME.

♡ ALWAYS,

KYLE MATTHEW DEL FIERRO

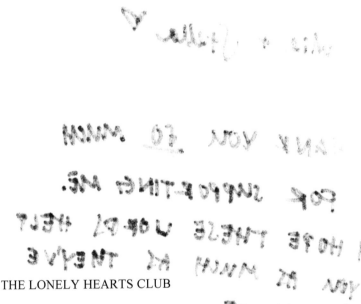

THE LONELY HEARTS CLUB

www.rewritereality.com

This book is a work of fiction. Names, characters, places, and
incidents are either products of the author's imagination or are used
fictitiously. Any resemblance to actual events or locales or persons,
living or dead, is entirely coincidental.

ISBN-13: 978-1984193001
ISBN-10: 1984193007

this is for you.

the lonely hearts club

"the worst kind of pain
often comes as a surprise
and wears the face of
someone you love"

prologue

My mother once told me about her life's great love. It was mid-summer. The sun was high in the sky and the days were longer. There was a light sheen of sweat settled on her skin and a serene expression on her face. Though nothing could take away from the pain in her eyes.

She met my father and just like children in a schoolyard, they weren't initially fond of each other, not even in the slightest. Though time passed and feelings changed. They fell in love and traveled the world together before giving up everything to come to America to start a family.

"I loved him so much, you know."

"Mom," I whispered.

"He always knew how to make me laugh, even when I was mad at him. That's just how he was. I could always count on him for a good laugh."

She tried desperately to hide the tears welling up in her eyes, but it was no use. I wrapped her in a hug and sat there, not letting my own tears fall —— I lost my father, but she lost *her first love.*

It was that… listening to the story of how my mom and dad fell in love, that made me wonder what my life's great love story would be.

1

seventeen

I remember it like it was yesterday. The way the music pulsed through my veins, how the room reeked of cigarette smoke and cheap booze. That was the first time I'd ever really been to a party.

You spotted me from across the hall, bent over a couch arm, spilling my guts into a plastic bag. I remember hearing nothing but the sound of your footsteps as you marched closer to me, red party cup in hand.

"Rough night?" you asked.

Though all I could muster up was a measly, "huh?" and before I knew it — you were gone.

I wiped the vomit off of my mouth and rejoined the party, though it felt like my presence was unnecessary. No one even noticed I'd been gone for the past twenty minutes. No one really saw me that night.

Except you.

THE LUST

it was instantaneous,

the lust

well, at least for me it was.

IN THE AIR

There was something in the air that night.

Something about the distance between you and I that made my skin itch like a mosquito bite that wouldn't quit.

I snuck into your bedroom. Tidied up before you got there in hopes of a reward. I washed myself with your soap, dried off with your towel, rummaged through your closet and picked out my favorite shirt of yours. You were always happy to see me wearing your clothes. They were always two sizes too large, but I knew that you would like it.

And so you found me, in your bed, waiting for you. How you whispered such sweet nonsense into my eager ears. How you undressed me with your eyes as your tongue worked its way towards mine. How your chest felt so warm against my back and how your hands locked around my wrists. Oh, how easy it was to peel away the layers of my heart for you.

PLAYTIME

how exquisite it is
to have a grown man
on his knees

FIRE

I'm afraid he's started a fire within me that will never die.
He's tempting and dangerous— but he's easy on the eyes.

A MIDNIGHT ADVENTURE

a midnight adventure,
a moment discreet;

walk in
don't speak
strip down
we meet.

a back door unlocked,
a bedroom ajar;

face down
eyes shut
stay still
have fun.

UNDRESS ME

the way you undress me
your lips laced with gin
so slow and so steady
i burn from within

CONVENIENCE

just like you wanted
i'm turned on; i'm indecent

a body on call
here for your convenience

INSTRUCTIONS

now wrap your hand around my neck—
                        make me scream,
                        make me cry,
                        make me moan,
                        make me beg.

now love me like you always do—
                        make it hard,
                        make it hot,
                        make it hurt,
                        make it cruel.

HIS LOVE

his arms
his back
his beard
his lips

his collarbone
his fingertips

his eyes
his nose
his tongue
his teeth

his love will be
the death of me

SMALL TALK

I was never good at small talk. You know, the sort of conversations you feel obligated to participate in? The cluster of words that seem to spill out of your mouth when you're trying so desperately to fill the silence— *small talk.*

But with you, I learned.

To find topics that might intrigue you. Movies you might've seen. Books you might've read. Restaurants you might've been to.

I learned what caught your attention and what didn't. I learned just how to lure you in and keep you there, just for a moment, long enough for me to remember everything. Every little detail. So that I could replay that moment over and over again in my mind.

Because in that moment, you were mine.

ACTIONS

"He loves me, I know it."

don't say it, show it.

ELECTRICITY

It feels like electricity's running through my veins when we're together doing nothing in particular. It's in the mundane moments. The stolen glances. The sporadic silences. It's those aspects that set my heart on fire. In all honesty, I'd rather do nothing with you than anything on my own.

AN ABRUPT ENDING

"This feels good."

You keep moving.

"This feels right."

You move faster.

"I love you."

You stop, you wait, you shiver.

FAMILIAR HANDS

it was exciting,
it was thrilling,
it was draining—

the feeling of familiar hands on me
of warmth and security and home
that was how it felt to be wrapped in
what i once thought was your love

A DYING LOVE

my fingers dance across your back
tracing the muscles; memorizing
it was in the afterglow where
i felt the closest to you, that
was where i misread this
where i misinterpreted
the signs that once
seemed so clear
and now seem
so foreign—
letters of
a dying
love

AT FIRST

you were gentle at first— careful not to break me
cause i was porcelain in your eyes; cause i was a
new toy on a shelf you were told not to play with

you were rough at last— and that i should've seen
cause boys like you have a taste for boys like me
just to use me and break me and forget all about it

SIGNALS

beads of sweat
race down my back
as if they're running
away from something

maybe they knew
that you were trouble
a warning in disguise
a cautionary force

how our bodies
send us these chemical
signals so quickly that
we end up missing them

eighteen

I found you sitting on your bed with your face buried in your hands. You looked up at me with bloodshot eyes and my stomach fell to the ground.

"What's wrong?" I asked.

You tensed up as I came closer to you.

"Hey. Come on, it's me. Tell me what happened."

Still, nothing.

I sat beside you on the edge of the bed and rubbed your back. I wanted you to feel safe, but you shivered to the touch. You wiped at your eyes with the sweater I gave you on your birthday and kept your head low.

Right there, in your bedroom where I gave you everything, where I let down my walls and invited you into my heart— four simple words gently spilled out of your mouth and destroyed my entire world.

"There was someone else."

BETRAYAL

nothing stings
quite like losing
your first love

THE NUMBER

27.

That was the number of times you tried to reach me. It was exactly 27 phone calls, 27 voicemails, 27 messages that were meant just for me.

That was how hard you fought for us. That was how much I mattered to you. That was how much you tried.

Though I wonder— how many times would you try to reach him?

RUINED

In the time that I spent picturing our life together and picking out the colors of our would-be wedding invitations, you were out with *him*.

And the whole time I had no idea *he* existed, you had no idea *I* existed.

So that night, I locked myself in the bathroom for hours.

I turned on the shower, sat in the tub, and let the water fall. I didn't even bother to take my clothes off because I didn't have the will in me to do anything other than just sit there. I didn't move, didn't breathe, didn't cry. I couldn't feel anything other than this gut wrenching pain in the middle of my chest. It was a heavy, consuming feeling. One so foreign, my body didn't know how to fix it. There was simply nothing left to fix.

It was too late. The damage had been done. There was no turning back.

You ruined me.

NAÏVE

i wanted to believe in love.
i wanted to believe in you.

but i was so,

      so

          wrong.

QUESTIONS

i want to know why
you ran for the trees
why you left me for dead
why you didn't want me

i want to know how
you can live with yourself
how you told all those lies
how you did it so well

i want to know who
could ruin our trust
who could be so unkind
who could do this to us

i want to know what
he'll do that i won't
what he can that i can't
what he has that i don't

NUMB

I lie in bed.

Stuck. Restless. Desperate. Lonely. Hurting. Wanting. Waiting. Aching.

My eyes are red, puffy, and dried out. My hair is greasy, my skin is oily. I pull the covers up to my neck and wrap myself in the warmth. It doesn't feel half as good as having a body to curl up into, but that isn't an option. I look exactly how I feel and I feel the same way I did when I left you—

Numb.

EMPTINESS

when you leave your trust
in the wrong hands
you end up with an emptiness
that was never there before

IN MY MIND

if you asked me to
i would run to you

how i always forget
you aren't so kind

if you longed for me
this would be easy

how you are always
better in my mind

THE SILENCE

it was in the silence
the lack of an excuse
the lack of any effort
where i found what i
had been looking for
i found answers to all
of my questions right
there— in the silence

CHILDISH

i shouldn't have thought
i could win at your game
the cards have been rigged
what a childish mistake

PUNISHMENT

I've thought about this moment for so long. I've dreamt about it.
I've let it simmer— this idea, this inkling, this desire for revenge.
See, I've waited for this moment. See, I rose up from the dead.

So, you will wait too, for the world to give what you deserve.

It'll be a long and painful wait;
But you will wait.
And you will hurt.

NIGHTMARES

I couldn't sleep for a while. I would wake up in the middle of the night screaming, crying, hurting. Droplets of sweat framed my face; my brows furrowed as I tried to remember the details that seemed to be missing. As if remembering how all of it went wrong would make the hurt go away.

It was a futile attempt to self-soothe; an attempt was all it was.

REMEMBER ME

i would've given you the world
if you asked me to
i would've figured it all out
just to comfort you
i would've given you my life
and my everything
but you still don't know
or love
or remember me

SAFETY

after you,
i sought out safety
in peculiar places

in libraries,
in coffee shops,
in unfamiliar faces

LONGING

a heart torn in two
still singing the blues

just a soul in the world
still longing for you

THE PAST

i still cling onto the past;

distant enough
that it's gentle
close enough
that it'll last

SEARCHING

i keep searching for something to fill this void
this pain that engulfs me
this need for love
or someone that might suffice
but i can't seem to find anything
or anyone anywhere
i just keep coming up short
i just keep searching

HEALED

i want to forgive you, i do

but time hasn't healed me
and it hasn't healed you

nineteen

There was nothing romantic about how we met.

It was hot, sweaty and crowded. Surrounded by strangers and entranced by the pulsing music, I found myself inebriated and drawn towards you.

We played a game of cat and mouse that night. Getting lost in the sea of dancing bodies, finding each other for a brief moment, then finding our way back into the crowd. And by the end of the night, I lost you.

It was in a dingy underground parking lot at two in the morning where fate decided to lend a helping hand. Stumbling towards my car with one of your friends holding you up, you yelled, *"Hey! It's you!"*

My fingers raced to roll down the passenger window. You stood there, your skin flushed pink and your smile so hypnotizing, in that moment—I forgot where I was.

"I don't know why, but we keep running into each other," you laughed.

I looked up at you with darkened eyes.

"I'll call you."

LOVE

a feeling
i thought was
lost long ago

a vibration
a sensation
i used to know

CATCH ME

i'm not afraid to fall in love,

i'm afraid of falling with
no one there to catch me

I F

if this is real,
          pinch me.

if this is love,
               kiss me.

if what we have
is temporary,

i beg you, please,
just warn me.

BUTTERFLIES

i thought i knew love
until you walked into my
life and said, *hello*

LOST & FOUND

the things i've lost
i can't recount
the misery
the fear
the doubt

the things i've found
i won't forget
the reverie
the love
i met

THAT'S IT

the numbness in your fingertips
the quiet rumbling in your chest
the way your legs tremble when
he calls your name the way your
skin glows beneath the moonlight
that's it— that's falling in love.

TO THE WIND

"I'm scared."

"Don't be. It's me. Come on."

I broke apart and stood there with my hands on your shoulders, steadying myself just long enough to think. Every situation and every possibility ran through my mind as I tried my best to think of a reason not to fall in love with you. But it wasn't the right time for reason and doubt.

It was time to throw caution to the wind.

DAYDREAMING

i catch myself
lost in the sunlight
staring at nothing but
thinking of everything

'daydreaming'
is what they call it
a common side effect
of a soul lost in love

INDESCRIBABLE

it's indescribable. it's a feeling
you can only feel. something
that no words or poetry or art
could perfectly describe. it's
something that you'll miss as
it first comes along. something
that you'll miss the second it's

gone.

ENDORPHINS

i feel a rush when you walk by
it's dizzying, this sudden high
it's puzzling that you can't see
the things your body does to me

A FLEETING LOVE

"Wait a second.

Just—let me take all of it in because it's never going to be like this again.

So, please, just wait a second."

THE SUMMER

at the end of the summer
in the backseat of my car
we familiarized ourselves
with each other's lips

in that vanishing moment
with my head in your arms
in that wonderful summer
you were the perfect fit

A COST

to be happy and in love
is all anyone really wants

but to keep it flourishing
there will surely be a cost

ALRIGHT

i hear this voice inside my brain
that's telling me to run away
you pull me in and hold me tight
and for a while it feels alright

ANSWERS

why do you stare into
my eyes as if you're
looking for answers

why am i so afraid of
what you might find
and what you never will

MEANT TO BE

I'd like to think that it was real. That all the time I spent with you added up to something. That all of our memories were like a single dot in an impressionist painting, and that there was more waiting for us. Though life doesn't hand you the truth gently. It's like being drenched in a tub of ice water. You see, things were off from the start— even I knew that.

But despite every argument I lost and every sacrifice I made for you, I chose to ignore the voice inside my head that was begging me to leave.

Maybe we're just not meant to be.

REALIZATIONS

The people who love the most often get hurt the most.

ENOUGH

tell me, is this love?

cause i think i lost my heart
i thought that we'd be closer now
but we feel so far apart

tell me, is this love?

cause it feels like something's off
is this how it's supposed to feel?
cause if so, i've had enough.

COLLECTING DUST

the romance dies the exact moment the love does.
it's like a candle without a flame, a lack of a spark
could render it useless. the love that dies lingers—
remaining still. occupying space. collecting dust.

twenty

"Why are you with him?"

"Do you love him?"

"You deserve so much more…"

Like sharp bursts of pain, her words pierced through me. Encapsulating my every thought, suffocating me, forcing me to wrap my head around the one thing I'd put so much time and energy into suppressing.

I spent that night crying in the backseat of my car— torn between calling you to take back everything I'd said and forcing myself to fall asleep. But I didn't sleep that night. Not even for a second.

I loved you.
I loved you.
I loved you.

Sometimes more than I loved myself. Sometimes often always.

But that night, against all odds, against the tears pouring out of my eyes and the frantic voice inside my head begging me to stop— I chose love.

Not for you, but for me.

HEARTBREAK

heartbreak won't break you
but the memories just might

LAST WORDS

i love you,

i cried,

but i need to love myself first.

OUR TIME

there is a time and place
to fall in love but it seems
as though our time is up

TOO LATE

When it's too late, you'll lose the will to fight for anything— even love.

YOU

i wanted the warmth the security the love
the mornings in bed the blurry nights the
kisses the butterflies and the laughs but
the one thing i didn't want enough was

you.

A PARTING PLEA

please,

stay,

i love you.

THE AFTERMATH

what used to be a safe space
has turned into a crime scene
our love was murdered here
in broad daylight— unseen

what used to be romantic has
become so awfully haunting
so desolate, so unpleasant
so bitter, so daunting

DREAMS

I sometimes go to sleep and dream about what we could've been. What might've happened if I hadn't given up on us so easily. And for the most part, I dream of a version of you that's so clearly not you— this "perfect man" that my subconscious has concocted on its own time, that the dreams don't seem to bother me. But every once in a while, I dream of you. The real you. The version of you that disagrees with me on everything. The version of you that laughs the way you do and smells the way you do and kisses the way you do. It's those dreams that hurt me the most. Because when I wake up, I always wish I wasn't dreaming.

I KNOW

i miss you,

i know
cause they always do
first it's this then
an empty apology too

i need you,

i know
cause they always do
it's too late now
there's no room in me
left for you

EXPIRATION DATE

i have yet to experience the
kind of love i crave so deeply

one that constantly gives back
one without an expiration date

PARASITE

You invest so much into another soul that the very thought of losing that love is terrifying. The fear of losing all that time and all those memories is like a parasite. It crawls into the deepest crevices and sinks its teeth into the most vulnerable places. It flows from within, like a slow acting poison— draining you so quietly you don't even notice yourself dying.

A DIFFERENCE

i still love him
but i'm no longer
in love with him

there's a difference
that my heart can't
seem to understand

A FINE LINE

There is a fine line between love and hate.

but still we danced along that line
we loved along that line
we died along that line

STILL THERE

there's still so much of you
flowing through me it's hard
not to notice it's hard not to care
some days i miss you so much
some days i need you like air
always at the end of the day
you're still there

A COMMON MISCONCEPTION

i've memorized your birthday and your favorite color. i know your phone number by heart. i still smell your cologne on freshly washed linens, long after your skin has left them. i still remember the sound of your voice just like i remember the lyrics to our favorite song. the worst part is that you're still the subject of my dreams and you probably always will be.

"it gets better" — a common misconception.

THE ONE

it's you who'll always be the one
who stayed and tried and fought for us
the one i should've left alone
the one i wish i didn't know

despite the pain, i'll tell the truth
i had to get away from you
i know how much you needed me
but you were not the one for me

THE ANATOMY OF MOVING ON

the muscles in my neck
are exhausted from
looking back

my teeth grind away
like the words i can't
bring myself to say

the bags under my eyes
swell and settle like
tears on empty nights

HISTORY

It feels like it never happened.

We were in love— an exhausting, consuming, dizzying, irrevocable love.

And somehow it still feels as though none of it happened.

THE LAST LETTER

if you're reading this, and i hurt you, in any way, i'm sorry.
i'm sorry for not knowing what to be sorry for. i'm sorry if
i ever made you feel less than enough. i'm sorry if i didn't
give you what you needed. i'm sorry if i didn't love you as
much as you loved me. i'm sorry for all the questions i left
unanswered and the space i built between us. i'm sorry for
the words. the words i used to heal. and the words i used
to feel; to feel anything more than torn. shattered. broken.
the words i used to hurt you. i'm sorry for the silence that
fills the air. for the emptiness when you hear my name. for
the urge to run in the other direction when you see me, for
not too long ago, things were different. in some aspects, we
ended up better off on our own. but sometimes it feels like
there's still so much we haven't done. but there isn't a *we;*
there's *you* and there's *me.* and i'm sorry. for making you
fall in love with me. for making promises i couldn't keep.
cause when i met you, you were like fire. hot. captivating.
dangerous. but when i left you, you were like glass. cold.
beautiful. breakable. and for that— i'm sorry.

TIME

time heals the wounds
we can't seem to fix
on our own

twenty one

Love surprised me that night.

Surrounded me with the people I care about the most. Kept me warm. Kept me happy. Made sure I was in the best possible state of mind that night because love had one last trick up its sleeve— one last surprise.

I spent exactly 35 minutes getting ready for my sister's surprise birthday party. I took a shower, meticulously fixed my hair, brushed my teeth, and rummaged through my closet to find something decent to wear.

Meeting you felt like drowning, like everything between us was a body of water and you were the air that I was trying so desperately to reach.

You were magnetizing. You were charming. You were deceiving.

You were different from the others.

Little did I know, you'd be the last man to break my heart.

LONELINESS

it is in the loneliness
where you will learn
to love the way you
deserve to be loved

THE PERFECT MAN

You checked off everything on my list.

Every physicality. Every personality trait. Every interest. Every hobby.

You were, ideally, *The Perfect Man.* And that's where it all went wrong. I built up expectations and became upset with the results. Because there is no such thing as the perfect man or the perfect love or the perfect you.

WE

We ended as quickly as we began.

With pretend excuses and pretend apologies and pretend forgiveness. Because there was nothing real about you and I. Everything was so finely fabricated; so carefully detailed that you'd miss the cracks if you weren't paying enough attention. We ignored all the warnings, no matter the cost.

We kept playing the game until one of us lost.

WANT

i want to
talk all night
but we never do
i want to believe
that you want
me too

i want to
stop wanting
all of these things
but the one thing
i can't help but
want is
you

THESE WORDS

it's sad but it's true
it's me without you
it's pretending to want
to welcome the new
it's this ache in my head
it's your side of the bed
it's the phone calls the
emails the texts left unread
it's pretending my heart
isn't breaking in two
it's pretending these words
weren't written for you

BROKEN

admitting you're broken
doesn't make you weak,

it makes you honest.

BEFORE YOU

I don't want to remember you.

I want nothing more than to wipe you from my memory. To move past this pain. To climb my way out of this trench you left me in and find the light. To find the courage to put myself back together again.

I want to remember who I was before you.

FINE

i'm fine,

what i mean is

you broke me.

LOOKING

no
i am not looking
for a partner or for love
i stopped looking
a long time ago
when i still had some hope
but those days are gone
it's much quieter now
and even if i was looking
i wouldn't say it out loud

FOREVER

nothing lasts forever—
what a tragic thing to know
    how it disappears
    like seasons
    how i wish
    it weren't so

nothing lasts forever—
why i wish i knew this then
    how this pain
    has taken over
    how i pray that
    this will end

THIS

i am used to—
being polite and
biting my tongue
and pretending i'm
fine and falling too
fast and wanting too
much and loving too
hard. i am not used to
this pain. this hurt. this
heaviness in my heart. oh,

i hope i never get used to this.

NO VACANCY

i've boarded up my windows.
locked the doors. shut off the
lights. shut out the world. i've
put up a sign around my heart
that says *no vacancy*. you see,
no one can break your heart if
they can't find it to begin with.

WHEN I THINK OF ME

It doesn't hurt anymore.

When I think of you, it doesn't hurt.

What hurts is when I think of me, and how easily I cracked. How quickly my confidence shattered at the sound of your name. How my knees got weak at the sight of your lips and how the goose bumps danced across my skin every time we touched. How I gave you all that power only for you to hurt me with it. What hurts is when I think about how lonely and empty and worthless I feel because you convinced me that I needed you.

What hurts is having to convince myself otherwise.

THE HUMAN HEART

the human heart is the strongest organ
but my heart's becoming much
weaker with time

always repairing the pain and trauma
left by men with hearts so much
weaker than mine

THE TOUGHEST WOUND

you were the toughest wound to heal
because you hurt me like no one else
because you were kind to me when i
needed it most because despite all of
my love for you it just wasn't enough

because i should have known better.

IN RETURN

you gave me hope but took it back. you gave me love but took it back.
you gave me memories but took it back. you gave me all of you but took
it back. so in return, i will give you poetry but unlike you,

i won't take it back.

THIS IS MY TRUTH

this is for the man who broke me.
for the man who made me feel like
i was anything less than enough.
for the man who made me think
i needed to be *a stronger man,*
an experienced man,
a man's man;

because of you, i am stronger.
but not in the way that you think.

i am stronger in the sense that
i have endured the greatest pain
of all and still made it out alive.

because of you, i am experienced.
but not in the way that you think.

i am experienced in the sense that
i drowned in the waves of your
inflicted heartbreak and survived.

i am experienced in the sense that
i have moved so far beyond you.

you really thought you knew me
but you skimmed the fine print.
because i am like a worn out book.

i am an honest man. i am a faithful man.
i know who i was and i know who i am.

this is it. this is my truth.

was that man enough for you?

WASTED

i have wasted enough time on you
enough lonely nights
enough solitude

so much so that i have lost myself
lost the happiness
lost the love i felt

ALONE

it's important to allow yourself
to be alone with your thoughts

it's the one place where there's
nothing to prove

REASONS

i began to look within myself
for the reasons why you left
what was wrong with me
what can i do differently
how can i fix this
but in that search i found something greater
and i will raise it in my hands
like a flag in the wind
i will shout it out loud
like a battle cry
i will wear it on my shoulders
for the world to see

you left because you didn't deserve me.

A LONELY HEART

hate will leave you in the dark

but

love will cure a lonely heart

epilogue

"For what it's worth, I still believe in love.

I believe in two souls lost in the world, finding love and finding home in one another. Love is boundless. Love sees past all of the imperfections. It happens right before your eyes and is often, if not always, uncontrollable.

Love hurts. It breaks you. Love makes it difficult to breathe when you're near the one you love. Love complicates things. Love makes you crazy. It will bring you to your highest high and back down to your lowest low and it'll leave you, in spite of all the pain, always coming back for more.

So maybe I'm not destined to have that once-in-a-lifetime love. Maybe the stars just aren't aligned for me— maybe the kind of love I desire just isn't in my cards. Maybe I'm destined to have a lonely heart," I sighed.

I took a sip of my latté and turned my eyes back to the book in my hands. Without hesitation, he reached across the table and tore the book from my grasp. I couldn't help but let out a laugh as he locked our fingers together and looked up at me with the softest of smiles.

"Join the club."

ACKNOWLEDGEMENTS

To my mother— for giving me life, teaching me how to be a kind man, and allowing me the freedom to follow my dreams.

The sisterhood; whose love, support, and friendship has never failed me. Through and through... I love you endlessly.

My beautiful and incredibly talented friends (you know who you are) without whom, this book might've never seen the light of day.

Lastly, to the past five years of my life: for bringing me the best of times and the worst of times. For encouraging me to write all of it down. You saved this lonely heart of mine— with love, tears, and some alone time.

ABOUT THE AUTHOR

Kyle Matthew Del Fierro is a screenwriter, poet, and creative blogger based in Los Angeles, California. After many years of taking various musical, dance and art courses, he focused his attention on his true passion— writing. Graduating with a Bachelor's Degree of Fine Arts in Screenwriting from the New York Film Academy, he has always been driven by art and storytelling through a multitude of creative mediums. Often recognized by his pen name: rewritereality, a minimal, structured aesthetic is realized on all spectrums through his work.

His first book, *The Lonely Hearts Club,* is a collection of poems and reimagined diary entries that have been cultivating for over five years.

INDEX

twenty

twenty one

join the club.

www.rewritereality.com

Made in the USA
San Bernardino, CA
22 April 2018